Meet Odie
A Paw Smart Book

By: D. S. Provance

Meet Odie
Text and Photographs by D. S. Provance
Design by A. J. Stawarz

All rights reserved. No part of this publication may be reproduced, stored in a retrieval system or transmitted in any form or by any means without the prior written permission of the author, except by a reviewer who may quote brief passages as part of a review.

© 2017, D. S. Provance
Crimson Gold Publishing

Remember, like people, dogs are unique individuals with their own personalities. This book is mostly about Odie.

Contact information:
inquiries@dsprovance.com
www.dsprovance.com

ISBN: 978-0-9986309-0-8

Dedicated to
Roni, Nava, Mckinley, Dallin, Afton,
Hannah, and Gretchen

Hi. My name is Odin, but friends call me Odie.

I am eight years old. I live in a blue and white house.

My yard has big trees and a goldfish pond with five fish. Some fish are shy and hide, but mine say hello.

 Dogs and fish come in many sizes. I am a big dog.

Fish may be smaller or bigger than you and me. They can be as small as peas or as big as school buses.

Paw Smart

Can you see my stripes?

Some dogs are orange red. Others are brown, black, yellow, or white. Some dogs have spots.

I am brown with black stripes. Any dog with stripes is called a brindle.

 Tigers and zebras have stripes as do many other animals.

Only dogs, cows, horses, and guinea pigs with stripes are brindles.

Paw Smart

My fur is thin and short.

It is perfect for summer, but does not keep me very warm in winter.

When I play in the snow, I wear a coat. Do you? My coat keeps me warm and comfy.

In icy or very cold weather, I wear booties to protect my paws.

My clothes are different from yours because our bodies are different.

Paw Smart

I know many words.

I know stop, come, sit, and go eat. If you say, "go look," I will run to a window to see what is in my yard.

I look because I am curious. Are you a curious person?

Some people think only puppies can learn new things. That is not true.

I am an adult dog, and I recently learned to "high five."

Paw Smart

Squirrels are curious, too.

I love my yard. Other furry animals do, too.

At night, you might see deer, raccoons, or a fox. During the day, I always see tree squirrels.

One squirrel family lives in a bird house and another inside a tree. Most live in nests made from leaves and twigs.

 Have you seen a squirrel?

Tree squirrels have long, bushy tails and run up and down trees. You might see them on the ground or jumping from tree to tree.

Paw Smart

I also always see birds and sometimes frogs, toads, and lizards.

Adult birds fly. Lizards can run up trees, and frogs swim in my pond. Toads hop.

These animals often eat mosquitoes, worms, or other insects. I do not eat such things, but I am glad they do. How about you?

 Did you find the lizard? It is a green anole.

Anoles will tilt their heads to look at you. They might be green or brown because anoles can change color like you can change clothes.

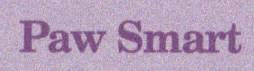

Do you like to walk and run?

I do! Sometimes I even jump like a kangaroo.

Every day I go for a walk. I meet friends and make new ones. I also explore. To keep me safe, I wear a leash.

Because I can only bark, howl, and whine, I wear a dog tag in case I get lost.

My tag tells people my name, address, and owner's phone number.

Paw Smart

I have lots of friends.

I first greet them with a special bark and a deep sniff to smell the air. Dogs sniff each other to say hello.

If you put out your hand, I would sniff you, too.

 Always walk, don't run at a dog. Some dogs are very shy and running will scare them.

Ask an adult first if you can pet a dog.

Paw Smart

I smell everything around me.

You read with your eyes. I mostly read with my nose.

My nose looks and works differently than yours. It lets me smell things you cannot. These smells tell me more about my world than my eyes do.

Sometimes dogs help find people who are lost.

By using its nose, a dog can follow footsteps you cannot see.

Paw Smart

You have a special smell.

Everyone does. No one smells the same to a dog.

If you wear a costume, you might fool my eyes, but your smell tells me you are you. You can't fool my nose!

Dogs know if their family is happy or sad. Your smell, voice, and posture change as feelings change.

If you are unhappy, I may try to comfort you.

Paw Smart

I am petted every day.

It makes me feel special like when you get a hug.

All dogs have a favorite petting spot. Mine is my bumpy, where my tail starts. Say "show me your bumpy" and I will.

 Do you know how to pet a dog?

Petting is the same as gently brushing your hair, but you pretend your hand is the brush.

Paw Smart

Beaches are lots of fun.

I love car rides.

They mean adventure! The car might take me to an ocean, park, or somewhere else fun.

The ocean has fishy smells, soft sand, and waves. The waves chase me and get me wet.

 Ocean water is salty and tastes yucky. You and I should not drink it.

Did you know whales and lobsters live in the ocean?

Paw Smart

At home, I play with my stuffed animals.

Some squeak. My two favorite toys are a blue teddy bear and a cat with a red bow. I often sleep with them.

Good night.

 Dogs see colors differently than you. We see blue and yellow, but not your red and green.

To me, my stuffed cat wears a yellowish bow.

Paw Smart

I have a snow beard.

 When I sleep, I dream. Sometimes I snore.

When I dream of playing, I may move my legs and paws as if I am running. I love to run.

Paw Smart

Glossary

Brindle: the name of a fur coat with patterns, usually stripes, found on dogs, horses, cattle, and guinea pigs

Bumpy: Odie's name for the area where his tail starts on his back

Costume: clothes worn to pretend you are someone else

Curiosity: asking questions to learn something new

Dream: what you see when you sleep

Explore: to learn something new

High five: an Odie trick where he puts the inside of his paw against the palm of a person's hand

Leash: rope that Odie wears on his collar and his friend holds by hand when they go for a walk

Odie (O-d): the nickname of Odin, a happy dog with his own book

Posture: how a person stands or sits

Snore: a sound a sleeping person or dog makes

Stripe: a line that is a different color from the parts next to it

Acknowledgments

My husband for recognizing our need for another family member

My parents for their love of dogs and books

Amy Stawarz for her amazing, award-winning graphic design skills

Linda Cale for her sharp editing skills

Janice Monaco of All Booked Up (Apex, NC) for her informative publication expertise

Daniel Dombrowski, D.V.M., of the North Carolina Museum of Natural Sciences (Raleigh, NC) for his wide-ranging animal expertise

Molly Stone-Sapir, CDBC & CDT, of the SPCA of Wake County (Raleigh, NC) for her perceptive companion animal behavior expertise

Our neighborhood friends for their book development insight and support:
Richard Adamski
Lesley Bradley
Margaret Griffin
Cara Nicholes
Greg Ward

Special Thanks

The Society for the Prevention of Cruelty to Animals (SPCA) of Wake County (North Carolina) rescued Odie from the streets when he was three months old. The staff and volunteers gave him love, taught him manners, and found him a good forever home. Odie enjoys daily walks, tummy rubs, and doggy cookies. He is a happy dog.

If you are considering adopting a new friend and sharing cool, fun adventures, please visit a rescue organization such as your local SPCA, other humane organizations, or county animal shelter. For suggestions, consider researching these websites:

www.guidestar.org/NonprofitDirectory.aspx

www.petfinder.com

dog.rescueshelter.com

www.animalshelter.org

www.ingramcontent.com/pod-product-compliance
Lightning Source LLC
Chambersburg PA
CBHW040331300426
44113CB00020B/2727